G

John Heath-Stubbs

GALILEO'S SALAD

CARCANET

First published in 1996 by
Carcanet Press Limited
402-406 Corn Exchange Buildings
Manchester M4 3BY

A CIP catalogue record for this book
is available from the British Library
ISBN 1 85754 260 6

The publisher acknowledges financial assistance
from the Arts Council of England

Set in 10pt Palatino by Bryan Williamson, Frome
Printed and bound in England by SRP Ltd, Exeter

Contents

Icarus

In memory of Adam Johnson 1965-1993

Daedalus the technician – he had contrived
Primitive machines for flying – two, in fact:
Helicopters or rather ornithopters
(Sealing wax, string, a parcel of feathers)
One for himself, the other for his son.

Thus they escaped, transcending
The labyrinths of law, Minoan stables,
Bull-running and furtively begotten
Twy-formed bestialities. They lifted themselves
Into the clear Aegean air. But Daedalus
Skimmed cautiously over the crests of the waves,
Like the shearwater, the bird of Diomed,
Or Ceyx, the fork-tailed tern. The boy meanwhile
Climbed higher and ever higher towards the sun,
'Father,' he cried, 'I see a naked man
Stand in that orb in the midst of the fire,
Twanging his golden harp strings. He is my lover,
And now I soar into his strong embrace.'

Daedalus had scarcely blurted out a warning
When the crash came. The wax melted:
Feathers dispersed in the air's turbulence.
Icarus tumbled out of the sky, struggled
For a moment among the waves, then sank.
The moray-eel and the dog-fish
Gnaw at his genitals, and the foul sea slug
Will rasp away his eyes.

It was far distant Daedalus made landfall.
He cast his wings aside, and tried
To chisel on cold marble blocks
His own achievement – cunning, ingenuity,
The triumph in the air. But when he came
To the depiction of his grief and loss
His hand faltered and the chisel fell.

Those who came after – refugees,
Traders or merely tourists, read
The scratched unimaged slabs.
They only said:
'These are the tears of things, the frozen tears
That drizzle in the heart, and touch
On the fatalities of men,
Of human beings that have got to die.'

* sunt lachrymae rerum

Vergil

The Ascent

to Peter Scupham

The summit of Parnassus, you thought
Should be severe and bleak but I'll remind you
When Hillary and Hunt ascended Everest
Their faithful Sherpa, Tensing, sacrificed
His last packet of chocolate
To the goddess of the mountain.
David Wright remarked, 'The only person
To behave in a civilised way on that occasion.'
But I am not at the summit yet. And if I'm spared
There'll be a few more steeps to climb before I get there: another
    volume,
These slight lines to you perhaps included.
The poems in my file are bleak enough,
Written in the knowledge one I loved,
My bright beautiful friend, had got to die –
And die before his time – and now is dead.
But I go on – there's nothing at the top
But the cold snow and the clear air –
Nothing between me and God except the darkness,
And the uncaring stars' predestined wheeling.

The Dark Birds

How I used to love those London crows –
Their raucous voices sounding
Over the mess of the post-war city.
I'd say, 'If there were truth in transmigration
I'd come back as a crow – there's nobody
That shoots them here, and plenty
Of rubbish for their dinners.'

But now it is as if they were pre-figuring
This town's decline, a final agony
That could be worse than Babylon or Rome.

They seem like those black birds, flying on devils' wings
Out of the void, to scoff
The dried up seeds of faith and hope,
Among the dust that strews
The too much trampled high-road of my life;
Or like that one that dogged the steps
Of Schubert's winter traveller trudging
Into the frozen heart of things –
A hurdy-gurdy wheezing on the ice.

The Flowers that Bloom in the Spring, Tra-la

In front of this house, which was once
A staid and bourgeois Victorian mansion, but now
Divided up into flats, the flowers
In springtime are blooming. It is the duty and pleasure
Of those who now inhabit what once
Was the servile basement, euphemistically known
As the garden flat, to tend and plant them.
The flowers have done their best, and we have had snowdrops,
Crocuses, daffodils, bluebells,
Lilac aubretia, and a few early roses.
They do not care nor know, these flowers,
That their annual entrée is no resurrection,
But simply recurrence, and not eternal recurrence either;
That they are laid out, perhaps
To deck our planet's funeral catafalque –
Or else a random wreath
For an Ophelia-crazy star who, drowning
In her own effluent, sings
Fragments of ancient ballads, foolish rhymes and songs –
I'd like to think I'd had a hand in them.

A Great Cosmic Cheer

A great cosmic cheer resounded
From star to star, from nebula to nebula,
Through the vast yawn of the godless universe:
Those hypothetical monkeys, chained
To their hypothetical typewriters,
In hypothetical infinite space and time, had signalled
They'd got the whole of Shakespeare typed –
Even down to spurious songs and sonnets
Mingled with truepenny in *The Passionate Pilgrim*.

Laughing Philosopher / Weeping Philosopher

I

In a goal-less caucus race,
Atoms rush through empty space
Or a lunatic dervish dance
From whose whirling, by mere chance
Order somehow comes to birth –
Sky and stars, and this green earth.
Living forms of every kind,
Till at length emergent mind
Gleams for a little while, and then
Things collapse to chaos again.
Old Democritus, how he laughed –
Scheme that's both sublime and daft.

II

All things flow. The primal fire
Smoulders in a cosmic pyre;
Nothing stays – day after day
Worlds are quite consumed away;
Soul's a momentary spark
Snuffed out in the ambient dark;
Elements to ashes burn,
Live each other's death in turn;
No man jumps in the same river
Twice – what's lost is gone forever.
Heraclitus had to weep –
Loss irrevocable and deep.

Galileo's Salad

Democritus, laughing philosopher –
Atoms dancing in the void. A maverick donkey
Wandered through the market place, helping himself
From produce stalls, until at length he came
Upon a booth, in which a skilful goldsmith
Had displayed his wares – among the rest
A marvellous gold platter, and upon it,
To indicate its function, a dozen or so
Of green figs had been placed.
The donkey scoffed these too – Democritus,
Who by mere chance was there, convulsed
In a wild paroxysm of helpless laughter.
It was his death – still guffawing,
As it disintegrated, his thin soul
Plunged in the meaningless void.

Galileo was ready for his supper.
He'd slogged all day over his books and papers
Tackling those atomists. At night his optic tube
Would sweep the sky, observing
Jupiter's satellites and the phases
Of mutable Venus – all the planets,
Our Earth among them, dancing round the sun,
Like priests that dance around a central altar.
His wife set down a plate of salad before him.
He gave a wryish smile. 'It seems,' he said,
'If what they'd prove is true, had lettuce leaves,
Radishes and cress and cucumber,
Salt crystals, peppercorns, and a fine dew
Of olive oil and vinegar, been drifting round
In empty space, since the beginning of time,
They would at length have chanced to come together
To make a salad.' 'But not,' answered his wife,
'One that's as fresh, well-seasoned and well-mixed
As this of mine is.' Later, he recommended
That remark of hers to his opponents.

The Dumb Ox

He didn't – (called 'the dumb ox') – talk much.
The silent brain was working, building
Syllogism on Aristotelian syllogism
The tremendous edifice of his 'Summa'.

Invited once to a dinner party – they had expected
Witty aperçus, even wisdom –
He sat, as course followed course, unspeaking,
Hammering out an argument. When the dessert came
He struck with a closed fist on an open palm –
Thwack! 'And that,' he said,
'Will settle the bacon of those accursed Manichees!'
At length, at the foot of the altar, he collapsed:
Granted a vision which made clear
All of his work was merely wind-vexed straws –
A deeper taciturnity he entered now –
The reticence of humility.

Until he drifted towards the ultimate silence.
His brethren came to his bedside. 'Father Thomas,' they said,
'You should keep your strength up. Is there any dish at all
That you might fancy?' The slow lips moved:
'You're very good,' he said. 'I think I could do
With some of those salted herrings –
The kind we get from England.'

At the Ninth Hour

And at that hour the sun was darkened.
A freak dust-storm blew in from the desert –
At the foot of the torture stake, Mary the mother
Stands in tears, and a young man bent with grief,
Called son of thunder, called the beloved.

In that unnatural twilit afternoon
The crowd blunders and stumbles
About the rubbish-tip, transacting
Quotidian business, murmuration of blowflies.

But those two, upon the skull-shaped tump,
Only hear the cry of dereliction,
Calling on God absconded through the darkness.

Three days away or three times three millennia,
The freshness of the resurrection morning –
Magdalen weeps before what seems
A violated tomb. Her sorrow,
In one bright flash, is suddenly transformed
Into the joy of recognition.

Light has rekindled in the darkness
That does not comprehend or overcome.

For the Shrine of Saint Edward, King and Martyr

'One for the road,' she said, 'a stirrup cup.'
He had mounted his horse at the castle gate,
And took in both hands the proffered drinking-horn.
He bent his head to quaff
The dark, sweetish, un-hopped ale,
A fifteen-year-old and king of England.

Then suddenly toppled forward, as the blade
Of the assassin's dagger thrust through his ribs.
The blue-eyed soul plunged downwards into a vortex,
Until a blood-red fiery angel seized it,
And yanked it up into a teenage paradise
Of apple-scrumping, ball games, beetle hunts,
Dressing gallantly, collection of trivia,
Impossible dreams of romance,
Unfeasible dreams of a purity that is perfect.

'We'll dump the corpse in the blind woman's cottage,' she said.
'If that old biddy should stumble upon it
She'll never know what she has fallen over.
Later on, we'll bury the carrion discreetly.'

But she was wrong – the blind pauper trod on the body:
A flash of light – light scarcely remembered –
Lit things up inside her one-room hovel:
Her wooden bowl, her horn spoon, her little jar of meal,
Her straw palette, covered with a moth-eaten goatskin,
Cold ashes of a fire and, blazing with miracle,
The broken body.

Incompetence, as always, is enthroned
(Then at Winchester, but it might as well be
Gotham or Troynovant) beggaring the realm
With acts of appeasement, danegeld;
Innocence lies in the dust.

One day perhaps my feet may dawdle down,
In my messy, half-believing, twentieth-century way
To those pathetic bones, where they are stowed,
With an Orthodox priest to serve them, and of course
Every appropriate modern fanglement –
Security-locks, burglarious alarms.

Balakirev and the Bugs

That brilliant amateur – he'd never studied
Harmony or counterpoint, but yet taught others
(A five-finger exercise of young composers),
A lifelong unbeliever, he suddenly improvised
God, as if he had stumbled on an unknown chord.
Gone were the images
Of Rurik's Russia, the breach in the wall of Tsargrad,
And Katya, pretty one, with black eyebrows,
That light also which sinisterly gleamed
Through Georgian darkness from Tamara's turrets,
Courteously inviting to an orgy – but at dawn
A body was flung from the battlements, down
To the roaring torrents of the Terek river.

But in his apartment the curtains were drawn,
The shutters folded. A closed stove burned.
The only light was from the lamps that gleamed
Before the icons, one in every corner.

Less and less frequently his friends called now,
Embarrassed by being urged to cross themselves
On every suitable occasion or unsuitable;
At being dragged off to attend the Liturgy,
On which their host evinced
Detailed, pedantic knowledge. Frowstily pious
Belledames, and an Old Believing priest
Seemed always there. But other little house-guests –
Bedbug, cockroach and the carpet-beetle –
Pullulated in the fug and the darkness.
If he caught one of them he would not kill it,
But took it to the window and ejected,
Piously murmuring: 'Go with God, beloved.'

I too have written some contingent verses,
Friendly towards such creatures. Now, as it were,
I cross myself and pray.
They do not issue from the darkened heart
Where sacred lamps burn down
Before the unavailing eidola.

The Bleak Midwinter

For the centenary of Christina Georgina Rossetti

Hesitated at the convent gate – could not relinquish
All the beauty of the natural world she loved:
'Winter the mother nurse of spring,
Lovely for her daughter's sake'; a small hairy caterpillar
That she might hold in her hand, the rainbow shell,
Paper nautilus that paddled upon tropic oceans.

Her only Aphrodite was a sea-mouse –
Marine worm preserved in a bottle –
Token of love from a rejected suitor.

'We are against thee, against thee, O God most high!' – those
        terrible words
From poor Algernon's *Atalanta in Calydon* –
A piece of paper was firmly pasted over them
In her copy of the book. Nor would she ever go
Into the British Museum mummy room:
The general resurrection could take place
At any moment. How awful if
Those dead pharaohs should break out
Of their sarcophagi, or sit bolt upright
In their showcases, leering and winking
With eyes that outstared nothing for millennia.

And so the road wound uphill all the way,
Though goblin voices whimpered and cajoled, protending
Forbidden fruit – nectarines, dewberries,
Oozing addictive sweetness – and at the end
Only a small room, a room for sleeping,
And the twilight that does not rise – or set,
Remembering perhaps, perhaps forgetting.

The prince dawdled, and the princess died.
Cancer wakened in the sterile womb.

O Lord come quickly, Christ that must be born
Into the bestial stable – ox and ass and camel
Into the bleak midwinter of the heart.

A Squirrel on the Window Ledge

'Look,' said my friend, cutting me off
In mid-sentence – I think
I was about to say something interesting –
'There is a squirrel upon your window ledge.'
And so there was. He'd come for bits of bread
I'd left there for the birds. Should I encourage him,
The silver-grizzled American interloper?
I know he's a thief, a garden vandal too –
But there are other ill-reputed guests
Who get my dole, the gluttonous louse-infected
London pigeon, and that study in black and white
Iniquity, the gazza ladra.
But let them come, and him as well!
I think he did too – come at first light,
Before I drew the shutters,
To pick up what I'd left the day before.
The birds, I fancy, would have swooped down at once
Soon as they spotted it. But he came furtively,
To stoke himself before the winter,
Through the long blessing of a mild November.
But now December's here, frost on its breath,
And he'll be holed up somewhere for the season.
Lie snug, shadow-tail, till the weather veers.

The Collared Dove

for Guthrie Mackie

'Dekaokto, dekaokto!' – it is a Greek voice
Among the English woodlands, shouting down
The foolish ring-dove, and the crooning turtle.

Hardy never heard it, nor John Clare,
William Cowper, Gilbert White, or Shakespeare,
For it exploded out of eastern Europe
Some four decades since or more, and now
The collared dove has crossed the Atlantic Ocean.

But when you saw one, a few days ago,
Feeding among the streetwise London pigeons,
Rufous and speckled, not dusty grey like them,
Exotic still it seemed, and a surprise.

Naming of Rivers

for Patrick Curry

Rivers in Celtic countries, or at least
Where those languages were spoken once,
Are just great waters – Avon or Usk,
Or else presiding femininities,
Nursing mothers of the lands they flow through –
The Irish Ban, and Anna Livia,
The Dee, divine one, likewise Milton's Sabrina,
The Don, who is the great goddess Danau;
Another mated with the Dagda on a water-course.
Danau took her name perhaps from the wide flood,
The Tanaïs, or else the Danube, where first maybe
The speakers of our linked and kindred dialects –
Indian and European –
Milked their flocks of ewes, herded their beeves,
Hunted with hounds the lynx, the bear, the beaver,
And the grey wolf; among the marshes
Cranes were calling, and the wild geese honked;
Within the beechwoods, wasps and midges
Tormented their bare skins.
      No less poetical
For being down to earth, the Saxon
Named his rivers from the way they ran.
There was the strong Stour, there was the Dart,
As straight as any arrow from the bow,
The hurrying Yar ('Yare, yare, good Iras'),
Windrush and Evenlode.

      Two sister rivers,
Watered that portion of the Southern county
I spent my boyhood in – the Celtic Avon
And Anglo-Saxon Stour. Once I paused
Upon a bridge that crossed the Hampshire Avon
To listen to the singing of the sedge-warbler
Among the reeds – a rapid song –
Sweet and harsh sounds jumbled all together.
It seemed as if in imitation
Of chattering waters as they tumbled onwards
Over smooth polished pebbles.

In Praise of Beans

Have you ever noticed how many Roman names
Seem to incorporate leguminous references –
Cicero with his chick-pea, Fabius with his beans,
Piso with his peas, and of course Lentulus
With his little lentil? How important
Those simple pulses must have been once
To the sons of Romulus – those square-jawed farmers
Who gaze through time from archaic portrait-busts,
More like mid-westerners than present day Italians
('The old Roman type,' Craddock Ratcliffe told us,
With a glass of sherry he would offer at tutorials,
'Nowadays is only found in the Trastevere').

They tilled the fruitful Ausonian fields,
Ploughed and sowed naked in the burning sun,
And then went home to their matronly wives
Who gave them garlic salad and a basin of beans.
They honoured the small gods of the fields, resented
Greek infiltration, Tuscan oppression – never dreamed
Sons of their sons' grandsons should rule the world.

Pythagoras and his lot looked askance:
'Eat beans,' he said, 'you might as well masticate
The honourable heads of your own grandparents!'
Ancestral spirits, metempsychosed,
Rumbling about in distended bellies
Concurred with his judgement in a flatulent chorus.

When the broad beans get tough, and the runner beans stringy,
The summer, we used to say, is over.
But now, what with crio-technology,
Not to mention the global warming,
We seem to have lost the seasons.

The Shield-Bug

An elegant little insect, green and crimson,
With slender legs, and a thin tapering beak,
Picks its way among the leaves and grasses.
This one is called a shield-bug – as you see,
His scutcheon is upon his back. Would you have guessed
Him pastoral kinsman of the gross urban bed-bug –
A foetid vampire, lurking
Till darkness summon him, behind
Cracked wainscots and the peeling wallpaper?

Midi

I think of you going south from Paris –
How once, for me, the train on a like journey
Stopped with a jolt, somewhere between stations,
And nowhere in particular. I had dozed off
After an early start, and jerked awake;
The sky and earth, it seemed,
Rang with the chirping of the cicadas:
The small, dumpy, homopterous bugs,
Membranes vibrating in their abdomens,
Drank the sweet juices from the leaves and stems.
Then I knew I was in the South, the treacherous sultriness
Of English summer left behind, and even
The Northernness and bustle of Paris. Like this might be, perhaps,
To jerk from death into another world –
But it's our own old sun that fosters here
The immemorial gifts of Earth –
Olive and vine, and, soon, the promised reaping.

il destrop !

Cimex Lectularius

It was in Devonshire we first met –
I was nine, or thereabouts – my parents
Had rented rooms for the summer holiday
In a picturesque country cottage. Picturesquely
Primitive it was, all right: an open sewer
Ran down the village street.
I was afflicted all those weeks
With great red swollen blains, much worse
Than any mosquito bites. No one, of course
Knew what they might be, though early one morning
I encountered you under the bedclothes –
Your squat brown body, your little beaky face.

Then there was Paris, after its liberation –
A cheap hotel on the left bank;
In Alexandria also, that apartment
You and the cockroaches rented. The only remedy
Was to try and sleep with the lights switched on.
(Cimex is lucifuge). But in the end
It was arsenical smoke bombs for the lot of you.

New York too, in the Bowery –
That garret I shared through a Christmas vacation,
Over the offices of a Chinese newspaper:
Winos sheltered in the downstairs lobby –
The stone floor was a-swim with their piss.

And now I most heartily hope
We shall not meet again. But, after all,
It was only one small drop of my blood you wanted,
And misery sometimes has acquainted me
With less honourable bedfellows
Than you, old comrade, little brother.

A Kind of Fly

There is a fly – just take my word:
It's something that I've read or heard,
Though where exactly I forget –
Which breeds inside a badger's set –
At first a grub, then by and by
Pupates then turns an adult fly
With gauzy wings to range the sky.

All-providing Mother Nature
Planted two instincts in this creature.
One was to take its rapid flight
Out of the den, towards the light.
But once there, in the open day,
Its other instinct comes in play –
To fly back to the badger's lair,
Shunning the light and spacious air,
To lay its eggs – for there its brood
Will find their shelter and their food.
So all its adult life, no doubt,
Is spent, so things have come about,
Just flying in and flying out.

Is there a human parallel?
Some people I know very well –
And so, I'm pretty sure do you –
Would seem to go their whole life through
In just such alternating flight
Between the darkness and the light.

Cerambus

for Francis Celoria

Cerambus on the mountains twanged
His home-made lyre, and blew
Across the bundle of slanted reeds
That was his pastoral pipe –
So sweet, so shrill the sound,
So blithe his singing,
The nymphs crept stealthily from the woods to hear him –
Hamadryads with oak leaves in their hair.
They loved him and were favourable, but he –
Familiarity bred contempt – in course of time
Introduced them into scandalous ballads;
They were no daughters of God, he said, and what was more
Up to all sorts of tricks. In our days
This kind of thing is provender for the tabloids.
They put their pretty heads together and consulted –
Then turned him to a hard-shelled boring beetle:
Boys cut his head off, use it for a toy, and he's the bearer
Of the dreaded Netherlandish elm-pox.

I knew a poet once, who started off
A young idealist, but then
He got into the wrong and fashionable set. Now
Critics of the Sunday supplements
Praise him – and he's not short
Of the odd bob or two, or so it's said.

As for our mythic hero,
He had his metamorphosis
And quite right too.

Wasted Prayer

Coinage once of poets, or potential poets
But now worn thin, and spat upon, and clipped – the clichés
Come rattling down the channels of the media.
I lift my eyes to the irresponsive heavens;
'Are there no leafless suburbs, is there anywhere
A medium sized, or even a large, old lady?
Can no ghost-hunter ferret out a genii,
Who without undue resistance, may be
Reinstated in his brassy bottle?'

Not All at Once

A poem should not yield
All its meaning at once. The Muse
Is not a kissogram girl on your doorstep,
Singing her trite greeting to a triter tune,
Sealed with a smacker. Rather think of her
As an accomplished mistress,
Economical with her favours – or maybe
The riddling bride of folk-tales. Failure,
Even slackness, solving her conundrums
Was death, was death at rising of the moon.

Homage to Marianne Moore

'Imaginary gardens with real toads in them' –
Your prescription for a poem;
But in my case, perhaps,
Three wise frogs
Who see no evil, hear no evil, croak no evil.

A Cold in the Head

Eight days sojourner with a sting in the tail –
My image of you is more or less Victorian,
Or remembered perhaps from Maeterlinck's *The Bluebird* –
A skinny little figure with a red nose,
A woolly nightcap and a flannel nightgown,
Bony feet plunged in a mustard bath:
Court jester to the Cave of Disease –
That conclave of ghouls, who crunch the bones,
Suck the blood, devour the lites and liver
Of suffering mankind. You slip out on furlough
In treacherous days of spring, or sneak along
Through the November fogs. Particularly, it seems,
You plague the English – that race, as someone said,
Born always two stiff drinks below par;
Lovers of stuffy rooms, contemners of garlic,
That inestimable dispersant of phlegm.
Here's for you then – a tot of whisky,
Hot water, Demerara sugar, cloves.

Redloam, My Ex

(Lileth loquitur)

He soon got bored with me, and so I left him.
I was cut out of the canonical books –
A folk memory only, night-monster, screech owl.
And he took up with that insipid creature –
Carved from an extra rib-bone so they say,
Havah or Hebe, whatever she called herself –
An apple-chomping amateur gardener.
They lost the lease of that garden – Redloam fathered
Those two boring boys, the one
Obsessed with his allotment, and the other
Always drooling over his livestock. You can be sure
That I was hiding behind a gorse-bush
When Cain struck Abel in the open field.

I'd gone, but he didn't know I was pregnant;
But I soon produced a multiple birth
Of Hobs and flibbertigibbets,
Leprechauns, spriggans, kobolds –
Most talented of all, my little gremlins,
Who can throw a spanner into
Redloam's clever contraptions, infect with viruses
His twittering computers.

But every now and then I come across
A boy who bears about him still
Something of Redloam's prelapsarian beauty.
I seem to each man like his own first love,
And when he's hanged himself, or drowned,
Or simply pined away, the autopsy being done,
They find a silken thread, one of my long gold hairs,
Twisted around the ventricles of his heart.

The God of Fun

The little god Bes – he was a parting present
When I left Egypt for the last time.
So he came back with me in my luggage –
Technically I committed an offence,
Bringing an antiquity out of the country
Without permission. But, through the centuries
He has got battered and broken a bit.
In particular, his feet are gone.
An artist friend made me a stand for him
And now his home is on a shelf in my flat
Along with other pieces of bric-a-brac.
Bes – a little pot-bellied African pygmy
With a big navel, but wearing on his head
The reed-crown of Upper Egypt imperial.
There are many pictures of him, dancing,
Or playing the harp, presiding at parties.
His image appears on ladies' make-up boxes –
A jolly god, the god of fun,
Among that rather po-faced company –
Osiris, Hathor, yelping Anubis.
Now he's got other friends here on this shelf –
A rather grim-looking Toltec sun-god,
Carved in volcanic glass obsidian;
A Nepalese lion that is also a signet;
The great goddess of Minoan Crete
Holding her serpents – or are they skeins of wool?

And a brass paperweight, after a bas-relief
Of none other than the Divine Cleopatra
Togged up the way that so much shocked Octavius –
'In the habilaments of the goddess Isis.'
These are tourist art – they have no souls,
But he has been the object of idolatry.
A Catholic friend says, 'Are you certain
You don't feel worried having him around?'
But I assure her there's no harm in him –
Little Bes, the fun-god, not so tall
As one of my two thumbs. So I don't bother

To have him exorcised, or things of that sort –
Although the small sad ghost
Of Jamie Bulger whimpers:
'Fun can get so easily out of hand.'

A West Country Story

As told by the Reverend Sabine Baring Gould,
and given by Jennifer Westwood in her book *Albion*
(Grafton Books, 1985)

A man was going home late – we'll call him Jack.
He'd had a skinful, but his legs were steady.
He strode out briskly and, as he maintained,
His brain was lucid, and his eyesight clear.
Suddenly, at a crossroads, he encountered
A pack of hounds – black dogs with saucer eyes
That sparkled phosphorescently. Among them
Was a tall huntsman, masked, also in black.
Jack knew who these were, but they didn't seem
To mean him any harm, so he called out,
Friendly like, as country people do:
'Had any sport tonight, sir?' 'Yes,' said the huntsman,
'You take this, Jack!' and flung a parcel to him,
Wrapped in sacking with flecks of drying blood.
'Thanks!' said Jack and went upon his way.
When he reached home, he lit a lamp to see
What he had got, and so unwrapped the parcel –
It was the body of his own young son,
Aged barely six years old.

In Memory

A scruffy beer drinkers' club, a basement
In a side street off the Charing Cross Road –
No introductions, and no names exchanged.
And then my room, a cellar
Under the pavement, near Lancaster Gate.
He spoke of the outback, of Ned Kelly –
A wild colonial boy with do-it-yourself armour –
Reproached me for my self-indulgent guilt.
'Nailed upon your private cross,' he said.
And, after that – it was not satisfactory:
Neither of us exactly young – for him
Only the second time with another man, he told me.

But, later on, I recognised
(I was in America) his photo
Upon the cover of a magazine.
Unmistakeable the balding head,
The battered face, broad shouldered stocky body.
I wondered if we'd ever meet again,
And if we did by chance, would he remember,
Or take it as a threat? But that
Was three decades ago and some years more.
And now a voice upon the air-waves tells me
That he is gone. He's dead and celebrated,
And then they played an interview
Recorded some years back. But residence
In England had quite sandpapered away
All the Australian vowels. But I am grieving –
Grieving for a little twig of love
That never blossomed – could not, should not blossom,
Among the débris of my journey's sidewalk.

A Memory of the Thirties

Of course I'd heard of it – the poverty, hunger marches,
The ignominy of the dole, the cruelty of the means test –
But hardly actual in our southern counties,
Our middle class townships. With other young people,
Before Christmas I'd go carol singing,
In aid of what were termed 'the distressed areas',
In ill-defined regions – Tyneside or South Wales.
In large houses we would be asked in, and offered
Mince pies and hot drinks.

Yet a touch of the shadow
Fell over all of us. My father,
Dying by inches, could not be a breadwinner; my mother
Daily slaved herself into exhaustion,
Keeping things together with her teaching;
Worry over small price differentials –
Nothing wasted, nothing thrown away;
Clothes patched and repatched.

And that cool day of early autumn
I saw a young man – not more than thirty –
(Probably less, but hunger had pinched him –
He could have had a wife and young children)
Singing or begging for pennies in the street.
His jacket was buttoned up in front,
But at his neck and throat I was aware
He wore no shirt beneath it. He had no shirt.

A provincial reader of rather old-fashioned
Poetry, I hadn't encountered
What were then the slick new school –
Modish revolutionaries, with their drawing-room Karl Marx;
Nor had I taken on board
The sexual mores of some of them.

But as I gazed at that young man
I felt a stab of pity and of shame,
While in my blood, my sixteen-year old blood,
Within whose torrent the hormones hopped and fizzed,
There stirred a craving for the naked flesh
Beneath the jacket and the threadbare trousers.

Upon Their Pedestals

Now that the twentieth century draws towards its end,
And I to mine, they're still left standing
Upon their pedestals – those three
Great jailers of the human spirit
Who once seemed liberators. But Freud
Has been observed to wobble, and Karl Marx
Is just a bit skew-wiff on his. At Highgate
The tears of heaven are falling now
On an unhonoured and unvisited grave. But Darwin,
Most boring and most honest of the three,
Seems screwed on tight enough. Huxley's monkeys
Hammer away at their typewriters. Cats
Are sporting in the clover. Though at his feet
The atom's dancing chaos,
And overhead the galaxies explode.

A Portrait by Reynolds   Laurence

A painter of surfaces, there are some will tell you,
More interested in clothes, than in the human being
Beneath the clothes, than in the soul
Within the human being. These clothes indeed
Are beautifully painted. They seem to shimmer
Under the English summer sun, as she stands there
In the great park. For her, a queen,
Such clothes would be informal, almost casual walking wear –
For us elegance, luxury. The castle,
That which at once marks and confines her status
Stands four-square in the background. She is not yet
That stiff old 'snuffy Charlotte' we have heard of.
You pass from contemplation of her dress
To study of the face – plain and dark-skinned
(This was an age dark skin was not admired).
The little eyes are kind, and there is pain in them.
Suddenly we remember –
It hasn't happened yet, but it will happen –
That she will see her husband
Turn horribly mad before those very eyes,
His own the colour of blackcurrant jelly.

For Dr Edward Lowbury on His Eightieth Birthday

It is the same god presides
Over the healing and poetic arts.
The seven-stringed lyre composes
The warring passions of the soul. Within the body's tetrarchy
In equilibrium the humours rest.

In putrid sludge and slime the deluge left
A serpent bred, as a baccillus might.
With one quick shot the Dorian archer
Slew it. There at the world's navel, the priestess
Chewed toxic laurel leaves, breathed in
The subterranean vapours, and then spoke
Political and ambiguous verses.

Apollo Smintheus, Lord of the Rats,
Despatched a plague through the Achaean tents.
His priest had been rebuffed, an old man weeping
Salt tears along the salt strand of the sea.

Physicians on Parnassus

To Edward Lowbury on the same occasion

Consider Thomas Campion and his lute,
Metaphysical Cowley, visionary Vaughan;
And those urbane Augustan doctors –
Richard Blackmore, Samuel Garth, John Armstrong:
Mark Akenside who walked the wards escorted
By orderlies with brooms to keep the patients off
('Stink and horror of the old hospitals!');
Angel-penned Goldsmith, the poor-Poll talker;
Apothecary and priest in one, tough-minded Crabbe;
Erasmus Darwin in his amorous botanic garden;.
And then John Keats, who diagnosed
His own warrant in the blood-tinged sputum;
Beddoes, for whom curare was
The final quip in Death's jest-book.

The Guinea Pig

'Pick him up by his tail and his eyes will drop out.' –
My father used to tell me. Nowadays
His names suggests other experiments:
Those who are tested for immunity –
For drugs, for novel surgical techniques:
The guinea pig boys. A sleazy club,
Somewhere off Shaftesbury Avenue, its décor
Suggesting a set for provincial production
Of Sheridan's *School for Scandal*. Once a year
It was the venue for their reunion –
Young airforce men, who in the war
Had horribly been burned, scalded, mutilated,
And now patched up by modern plastic skills –
Shadows of lost beauty, shattered youth,
Peeped out behind the renovation-jobs.

He's nothing to do with Guinea, and he isn't a pig.
The Restless Cavy, to give him his full title,
Is a tailless Andean hystricomorph rodent.
When once the heaven-descended Incas
Ruled an empire which stretched all the way
From Bolivia to the utmost tip of Chile,
Clad in soft mantles of vicuna wool
(Worn once and then discarded)
Their subjects fed mainly upon potatoes –
Left out in the high mountain cold to freeze rock hard,
Then pounded with a mallet. Extra protein –
Cavies scampered about inside the one-roomed huts:
Scrag one, and skin him, and put him in the stew.

The campesinos now, I wonder
If they fare even as well as that;
In their remote villages, waiting
Till soldiery arrive, disguised
As senderistas, or
The senderistas posing as the troops –
'Hang them up by their heels, and flog them,
And their eyes will drop out.'

Cat Star Rising

After the malice of Hermann Goering,
And rabies of Adolf had done their worst,
Vomiting fires from heaven upon
The beloved city, strafing
The shrines of God, Sir Christopher's stone poems,
There came a time for clearing up the mess,
For reconstruction. In the foundations
Of one of those churches – I do not now remember
Which of the saints Omnipotence had permitted
Not to intercede for its protection –
They found the mummified corpse of a poor cat
Who had been buried there – buried alive
Three centuries and some decades ago
As a foundation sacrifice. Freemasons
Had bricked it up, solemnly singing
Hymns to fraternal love – not ones by Mozart –
He hadn't been born yet – but someone or other,
Let's hazard Jeremiah Clarke (poor Jeremiah
Who was to shoot himself, and lie
In an unhallowed grave).

The dried-up skull and bones and catskin lay
On the construction site. But when night came
Two cherub kittens, terms of the angel tiger,
Alighted there and said,
'Poor Tom, we've come to take you home.
Your sentinel duty here was long enough –
But the suffering might have been worse – you could have been
One of those cats that were roasted alive
In hollow iron effigies of the Pope.
Out of the gaping mouth tormented screams
(Anticipating Francis Bacon)
Of an incinerating cat proceeded,
In times of anti-Papist feeling. Now we'll take you
Up to the Cat-Star. "Where is that?" you ask.
In a far distant quarter of the sky
From where Orion plays the toreador –
The giant generated out of urine, followed
By his two yowling dogs, Sirius and Procyon.

46

There you shall sport in thickets
Of catnip and Valerian. Where milky fountains gush,
And there are pools of gold and silver fishes
More glistering than the ones that lured
The pensive Selima to her watery grave.
Fluffy pink and white mice dance about
Singing and whistling "Catch me if you can!" –
And of course you always do. And in those groves
Our Lady of the Cats –
The Northern Freya, Pharaonic Bastet,
Purringly presides – with seven handmaidens
Damozels, whose seven secret names
Are seven sweet and caterwauling symphonies.'

It was chucking out time in London. From the pubs
Of Soho, Chelsea, Notting Hill and Limehouse
Drunkards came reeling forth. But some marked in the sky
Six small green points of light, six shining meteors,
Which, contrary to every law of nature,
Known and unknown, rose ever upwards
Until they reached an undiscovered star.

The Expostulation of Arfur, the Lion

I'm called Arfur – I'm a lion,
My lineage ancient, but no scion
Of those Ethiopian growlers,
Yellowish-brown savanna prowlers
With names like 'Elsa', for my clan
Roamed the vales of Hindustan.
We survived while history winked
Deemed at one time quite extinct.
In Rome's imperial heyday we
Were often brought to Italy;
Lions were in great demand
For combat on the arena sand.
The Coliseum's floor was red
With martyr's blood that had been shed,
In witness of their faith and truth.
Round about the glassy sea
Saints praise the Lord – he set them free,
Using their terror and their pain
They bless the lion's gory mane.
Now, in a more kindly age
I'm not even in a cage,
But an enclosure at the zoo
For the enlightened crowd to view.
I get a decent meal to eat
Each afternoon, of good red meat,
Life I find is fairly boring
I spend a deal of time just snoring
(They have provided me a den) –
But I get really furious when
A member of the human race
Invades my territorial space.
Only just the other day
One roused my anger in this way –
He climbed the fence, and took his stand,
Reciting texts, Bible in hand –
But one text he forgot – (Poor sod!) –
'Thou shalt not tempt the Lord thy God.'
He thought he was the prophet Daniel
And I'd be tame as any spaniel.

All at once I pounced on him,
Would have torn him limb from limb,
But the keepers rushed in, banging
Dustbin lids, and at that clanging
I let go. They deftly snatched
The simpleton away. He's patched
And plastered in the hospital –
Nurses at his beck and call.
There ran a rumour through the town:
'That lion ought to be put down.
We should aim a lethal dart
Into his nobly-sounding heart.'
Others, luckily for me,
Will not accept this strategy,
Saying, 'He's the beasts' High King,
Only doing his own thing.
Let him do it. But, no doubt,
We must keep intruders out.'
Now I've got a loftier fence
Excluding *homo sapiens*,
Who, like all the other apes
Is always up to foolish japes.

Balaeniceps Rex

The shoe-billed stork, balaeniceps,
Proceeds with slow deliberate steps
Through marshes round about Sudan
Regions not much explored by man.
The other swamp-birds, wading by,
Or swimming, with a wary eye,
Know that his formidable beak
Can give a quite unpleasant tweak.

It seems a kind of arrogance
Informs his tall and stately stance,
As if he knew himself to be
A paradox of taxonomy;
For which is his authentic clan –
Heron, or stork, or pelican?

Sometimes, though this is rather rare,
He spreads his wings and mounts the air,
As seeking to extend his range;
But his appearance is so strange
That some suppose that they descry
A pterodactyl in the sky.

Why do I write this stuff? My muse
Inclines at present to refuse,
And when that lady needs a stand-in,
Writing mere verse can keep one's hand in;
And for Balaeniceps, maybe
I have a kind of sympathy –
I too will not be classified,
And have my own peculiar pride;
Though beakless, I too when I please
Can sometimes tweak my enemies.

The King of the Cats

To the memory of George Barker 1913-1992

When Yeats first heard that Swinburne was dead,
'Now I am the king of the cats!' he said.
I know the story to which he referred –
A tale perhaps you've already heard.
There are several versions – I'll tell you one
That I remember. I think it's quite fun.

Through hours of darkness a traveller strode
Along a weary and difficult road.
Black clouds had veiled the moon's clear light
As he walked on through a stormy night.
A fierce wind blustered, rain pelted down –
He'd miles to go till he reached the town,
But there he knew that, in the end,
He would find the hospitable house of a friend,
Warmth, good food, and a well-aired bed,
And a down-stuffed pillow for his head.
Then all of a sudden, a lightning flash –
Hard on it, a sickening thunder crash –
Lit up the sky. For a moment, it showed
An impressive pile not far from the road.
Deserted now, and dilapidated,
It had once been an abbey, much celebrated
For learning, and for piety too,
Manned by a sturdy monastic crew.
But the brethren long were dispersed and fled,
And the tall roofs had been stripped of their lead.
But some kind of shelter one still might gain
Within those walls, from the wind and the rain.
So our traveller turned inside, to wait
Till the elements' fury should abate,
Till the pelting rain and the stormy blast,
And the thunder and lightning all should be passed.
But as he sheltered there through the night
He beheld a strange and mysterious sight.
A procession of cats came winding along
With a sorrowful caterwauling song;

51

And to punctuate that sad singing
Somewhere a bell was mournfully ringing.
In the midst of them all were four great gibs,
As black as midnight, with snowy bibs.
They bore a small coffin, and on it a crown
Of gold. And they solemnly lowered it down
Into a deep dark hole in the ground.
Then all of them set up a wailing sound.
It ceased, and they silently melted away
Into the night, where all cats are grey.
Then the traveller saw that the storm had passed by –
There were streaks of dawn in the clearing sky.
Once more he hopefully took the road,
And soon he arrived at his friend's abode.
As he sat by the fire with a cheering glass,
He related all that had come to pass,
With those strange rites in the ruined abbey.
But as he did so the family tabby,
Curled up on the hearth-rug, opened one eye,
And said in a human voice, 'So I
Am now the king of the cats!' And that
Was the last they ever saw of the cat –
For up the chimney that moggy flew,
As fast as a puff of smoke might do.

Now to return to what Yeats said
When they told him Algernon Swinburne was dead –
When I was young, there could be no fuss
As to who was the king of the cats for us.
There was only one great Tom, and he,
Puss or possum, was TSE.
When his ashes were laid to rest in East Coker,
The king of the cats had to be that joker
Wystan Auden. When he snuffed out,
For my pals and me, there could be no doubt,
Whatever dusty old dons might say,
George Barker was king of the cats that day
(But a barker of course is really a dog –
And dog spelt backwards is God's incog).
Now he has been taken, I look around,
And ask where the king of the cats may be found.

What I mostly see is a litter of kittens,
Who handle poetry with woolly mittens;
They chase their own tails, they worry small rats –
But where's the undoubted king of the cats?

Tom Bawcock's Day

for Charles Causley

> *'Tom Bawcock was a Mous'ole man –*
> *At least that's how the story ran:*
> *A better fate you could not wish –*
> *To dine on seven kinds of fish.'*   Anon.

Death to our best friends! – a mighty cry
Reverberated to the arching sky.
In Newlyn, or Polperro, or St Ives –
There were both men and boys who'd risked their lives
Before they'd hauled those best friends to the land.
Those best friends were, as you must understand,
The teeming mackerel with their stripes of blue
Which every season as a tribute due
Swam in upon the all-prolific sea
To give to Cornwall its prosperity.
And next the shout was 'Long life to the Pope!'
These pious Methodists presumed to hope
While in St Peter's chair a Pope might reign
His rules of abstinence should be their gain –
In Lent, on Fridays too, that Catholic bunch
Would still eat fish when they sat down to lunch –
Though Protestant Cornish thought it all my eye
And any day could have star-gazey pie
Where the poor fish their little heads would thrust,
To stare at heaven, through a pastry crust.
And after that a third prodigious shout –
'May the streets run with blood!' came ringing out
To mark the time when fishes' guts were slit –
The surplus catch, those that were judged as fit
For salting or for smoking, and then packed
In sturdy barrels, all for export stacked.

Those cries were heard a while ago. The seas
Are not so bounteous now. Our greed
And our bad husbandry have bled them.
The puffin and the guillemot are starving, and we shoot
The beautiful seals, for taking
No more than their just share.

Rexque Futurus

Under some bronze-age tump, or iron-age hill-fort,
Arthur and his company are sleeping.
Awaiting the reveillé that shall summon
Them to the final showdown.

It must be most unlucky, I'd surmise,
That any heir of England's royal line
Be christened 'Arthur', till
The true one come again.

Arthur of Brittany – his broken body
At the foot of the battlements; Arthur Tudor,
No more than a schoolboy likewise, left behind him
Through his marriage, consummated or else not,
To Kate of Aragon, a mort of trouble
We haven't cleared up yet. But I, for my part,
Will say God bless the Prince of Wales,
Charles Philip Arthur George, and God preserve him
From what the first Elizabeth's Edmund Spenser named –
'Envy, detraction and the blatant beast'.

1994

A Ballad of the Piltdown Man

The Piltdown man, the Piltdown man –
   He was a hunting type, I guess,
Who, with a pack of Surrey pumas,
   Pursued the monster of Loch Ness.

And once, when a blue moon was shining,
   He, on a mystic Druid stone
Inscribed the lays of Ossian (with
   A dedication to Pope Joan).

The Nightingale and the Rose

'Really, this kind of thing gets up one's nose!
Can it make any sense – would you suppose? –
    That mindless twittering of the nightingale,
Infatuated with an opening rose?' –

So said the starling to her friend the rook.
They went to search for maggots. But it took
    Omar to mark the nightingale, while still
He drank, and murmured verses without book,

Until the rising moon began to shine:
That self-same moon tonight is yours and mine –
    No nightingale may sing in Berkeley Square,
But we've good talk, good company, good wine.

For the Centenary Dinner of
the Omar Khayyam Society

When Omar scrutinised the midnight sky,
He marked the starry wheels send spinning by
The days, the months, the seasons and the years,
And centuries in the twinkling of an eye.

A hundred years have passed since first they met –
The founders of our feast. The places set
For them are ours tonight. They have departed,
And we are bound to join them. Others yet –

Star-scattered guests shall come, and gather here,
When in the spring or fall new moons appear,
New broods of nightingales rehearse their songs,
And new-blown roses sweeten all the air.

Twelve Festival Poems
(For the young)

NEW YEAR'S DAY

Jack made a New Year's resolution:
'Every morning a cold ablution!'
But, came January the second
Hot baths were really best, he reckoned,
For his fragile constitution.

ST VALENTINE'S DAY

Today the small birds choose their mates,
And boys and girls fix up their dates:
Although, odds are, the sun won't shine,
Good morrow to you, Valentine!

My Love, if it should rain today,
We will not take the woodland way,
But find a cosy place to dine –
And you'll still be my Valentine.

SHROVE TUESDAY

At Olney there's a pancake race –
Housewives think it no disgrace
To compete. They have such fun
Tossing pancakes as they run.

MOTHERING SUNDAY

Mid-Lent, and Mothering Sunday's come –
A bunch of daffs for good old Mum.

EASTER DAY

Jesus bursts His tomb. Young chickens
Break their eggshells – new life quickens
And a jolly Jack hare jumps down from the moon
Bringing us chocolate eggs for a boon.

ALL FOOLS' DAY

Egbert the Egg-head knew zoology,
Teleology, and geology,
Etymology, entomology,
And every other species of ology.
When the rest of the boys were playing games
He was learning up lists of Latin names,
Watched high-brow programmes on the media,
Or burrowed through the encyclopaedia,
Studying heat and light and sound.
But when All Fools' Day came around,
A boy called Dickie Dunderpate,
Consumed with jealousy and hate,
Played a decidedly nasty trick –
If you want my opinion, I think it was sick.
Secreting an earwig in Egbert's bed,
He said it would burrow inside his head –
With pincers, and feelers, and squiggly legs,
A female earwig, heavy with eggs.
Dick Dunderpate said they were ready to hatch,
And the little earwigs would scrabble and scratch,
And scamper around in poor Egbert's brain –
Then tunnel their way to the light again.

Of course this tale was quite absurd,
But Egbert believed Dick's every word.
I really think he'd have died of shock,
If it hadn't all ended at twelve o'clock,
When every obnoxious boy in the school
Shouted out, 'Egbert's an April Fool!'
Now of the characters in this story,
One ended in shame and the other in glory:
Egbert, with all his remarkable knowledge,
Was elected the head of an Oxford college –
Revered, though none of them quite understood
His books, alike by the great and the good.
But Dickie, who had devised this lark
Turned into a dull pen-pushing clerk;
But he had become such a horrible slob
He couldn't even hang onto that job,
And peddling shoelaces in the gutter,
Earned a crust – but hardly his bread and butter.

ST GEORGE'S DAY

In coils upon the desert sand
    The Dragon is lying dead:
Saint George had driven his sharp spear through it,
    And then cut off its head.

The beautiful eastern princess, Sabra,
    Whom the monster had hoped to eat,
Did a triumph-dance to the tinkling sound
    Of the anklets on her feet.

We'll celebrate Saint George's Day
    With wholesome English cheer:
With solid boiled suet dumplings,
    And with roast beef and beer;

And wear red roses in our hat-bands:
    A mark of homage, due
To George the dragon-slaying martyr –
    And sweetest Shakespeare too.

MAY DAY

Robin Hood in Sherwood lay:
'Down in Nottingham today
They celebrate the first of May.'
Maid Marion said: 'I will go down
To the hubbub and dust of Nottingham town –
I know they'll grant me the May Queen's crown.
There'll be dancing around the May Pole tree,
And every eye will be fixed on me.
While the fiddler is playing his "Fiddlededee!"
And the shawms and the trumpets are braying loud,
You boys can mingle with the crowd
And pick the pockets of the rich and the proud.'
Then Little John, Robin, Will Scarlet and all,
Concurred in the plan: 'Before darkness shall fall,
With luck on our side, we'll make a good haul!'
'Of course they gave it all to the poor –
To the beggar who lay at the Sheriff's door,
And the dear old lady they'd helped before,
Who lived alone in her squalid hut?'
You've heard that that was their custom – but
I think it likely they took their cut.

Moral

If someone maintains that you can thieve
From goodness of heart, I say (though I grieve
To tell you) that's someone you shouldn't believe.

MIDSUMMER EVE

Steal from your house at the midnight hour –
This is a night of magical power,
When the blossomless fern bears a golden flower,
And you are to cull its miraculous seed.
That your hands and your heart be pure, take heed,
And all good spirits your task shall speed.
Invisible then, by forest and stream
You will wander beneath the moon's soft gleam –
And wake in the morning, to think it a dream.

ALL HALLOWEEN

Ugly witches can be seen,
Doubtless, upon Halloween.

In the North, if I'm told right,
Children call it 'Mischief Night'.

They go round from street to street,
Threatening all with 'Trick or treat!'

Which do people dread the more,
Hearing knocking at their door –

Children with collecting bags,
Or the ghastly midnight hags?

GUY FAWKES DAY

Fifth of November, and you will remember
An unsuccessful political plot:
If you were thinking of blowing up Parliament
Guy Fawkes' ghost says, 'Much better not!'

Good Prince Albert said to the Queen:
'The rooms, resplendent with evergreen,
Holly and ivy, make a show –
Along with the pagan mistletoe.
Down in the kitchens, the cooks have boasted
Of geese and turkeys duly roasted,
And a grand boar's head to great applause
Borne in with an orange between its jaws,
Of Christmas puddings in a brandy blaze,
Mince pies, by the dozen, for the Twelve Days.
There's one thing only to make complete
This our seasonal family treat –
And that is a really good Christmas tree:
I knew them from boyhood in Germany.'
Then the Queen gave orders – before it was dark,
A tree was selected in the royal park;
It was a good straight Douglas fir,
And was brought to the Queen to be passed by her,
And then set up in a tub in the hall,
And hung with many a glittering ball,
With silver bells, and with candles bright,
And an angel-doll at the topmost height,
With a gilded halo, and blowing a horn
To announce to the world that Christ is born.
Then the little princes, and the princesses
With tinsel wreaths in their flowing tresses,
Danced in a ring, with laughter and glee,
Around that wonderful Christmas tree.
Then one of them said: 'Time passes too soon –
Let us crown our joy with a happy tune.
Dearest Papa, now won't you play
The piece you composed just the other day –
It's even prettier than the one
You played with that nice Mr Mendelssohn!'
Then good Prince Albert, with modest pride
Tootled an air on his ophicleide.